Health and the Income Inequality Hypothesis

A Doctrine in Search of Data

Nicholas Eberstadt
and
Sally Satel, MD

The AEI Press

Publisher for the American Enterprise Institute

WASHINGTON, D.C.

2004

To order call toll free
1-800-462-6420 or 1-717-794-3800. For all other inquiries please
contact AEI Press, 1150 Seventeenth Street, N.W., Washington D.C.
20036 or call 1-800-862-5801.

Library of Congress Cataloging-in-Publication Data
Eberstadt, Nick, 1955-
    Health and the income inequality hypothesis : a doctrine in
    search of data/ Nicholas Eberstadt and Sally Satel.
        p. cm.
    ISBN 0-8447-7169-4 (pbk.)
    1. Income distribution. I. Satel, Sally L. II. Title.

    HB523.E34 2004
    339.2—dc 22

                                                      2003067301

1 3 5 7 9 10 8 6 4 2

ISBN 978-0-8447-7169-4

1 3 5 7 9 10 8 6 4 2

Contents

Illustrations

Acknowledgments

The authors would like to thank Mr. Henry Wendt and the W. H. Brady Foundation for their generous support. Jeffrey Milyo of the University of Chicago provided invaluable scholarly insight. We extend our warm thanks to Juyne Linger, who edited the manuscript; Heather Dresser and Lisa Howie, who prepared tables and figures; and Nell Manning, who assisted with the manuscript.

1

Introduction

Few would take exception to the proposition that an improvement in the material well-being of the poor would enhance not only their living standard, but their health levels as well. A number of influential recent studies, however, purport to show that inequality in income—not poverty per se—has detrimental health consequences. This "inequality hypothesis" is meant to apply to everyone, regardless of wealth or social standing, and predicts that the risk of illness depends upon whether one lives in a society that is stratified or egalitarian. Thus, according to this hypothesis, while the poor may suffer the most from inequality, the better off and even the rich suffer as well.

This is a dramatic claim—and one with potentially far-reaching implications. It extends far beyond the current paradigms upon which contemporary Western social welfare policy is premised. Current welfare policy, after all, posits that overall national health can be improved by transferring resources from society's more affluent members to its poorest and most vulnerable groups. The inequality thesis, by contrast, would seem to suggest that simply taking wealth away from the rich—and thereby reducing measured economic inequality—should *in itself* produce an improvement in national health. Indeed, the inequality thesis suggests that, all other things being equal, a cutback in the income of the well-to-do could be expected to improve the health status of the poor, and possibly the rich themselves—even if society were left with a lower average income level as a result of those cutbacks.

Proponents of the hypothesis have offered a number of possible mechanisms for this claimed relationship. Hierarchies, for

1

example, may increase stress levels, which can lead to heart disease or self-destructive behavior. Again, those at the bottom of the economic or social ladder would feel the greatest effect of this stress, but even those at the top would experience some impact. Another possibility might be that inequality causes people to perceive their neighbors as more alien or less trustworthy than would be the case in an egalitarian society; as a result, citizens would be less concerned about the welfare of their neighbors.

The inequality hypothesis has fast become conventional wisdom among many medical sociologists and public health scholars. For example, in *Unhealthy Societies: The Afflictions of Inequality,* Richard G. Wilkinson of Nottingham University Medical School argues that income inequality is "one of the most powerful determinants of health" and "the most important limitation of the quality of life in modern societies."[1] The academic world is by no means immune to fads, but the sudden popularity of the inequality hypothesis—in schools of public health; in scholarly journals like the *American Journal of Public Health;*[2] in institutions such as the American Public Health Association;[3] and in health philanthropies like the Robert Wood Johnson Foundation[4]—is quite extraordinary. One reason the hypothesis may have proved so compelling in academia is that it points toward a social reform long favored by egalitarians—the redistribution of wealth. In view of the new and now well-documented activist mission of many schools of public health—that is, to promote social justice—it is not surprising that public health circles might react enthusiastically to a thesis that would seem to support their own preferences for an expansive social and economic policy agenda.

In the last few years, the notion that inequality is bad for health has surfaced in political discussions, taxpayer-funded policy research fora, and the popular media. British Prime Minister Tony Blair has stated, "There is no doubt that the published statistics show a link between inequality and health."[5] The World Bank has dedicated a web page to the inequality hypothesis.[6] In the United States, the National Institutes of Health, Centers for Disease Control and Prevention,[7] and reporters for the *New*

York Times and *Washington Post,* among others, have given favorable coverage to the subject, implying that the hypothesis has become accepted wisdom among public health researchers and epidemiologists.[8]

But the enthusiasm of many researchers and observers goes well beyond what might be warranted by the weight of the evidence alone. A very persuasive, if less publicly heralded, body of scholarship that challenges the inequality hypothesis is currently emerging.

In this analysis, we present both sides of the debate by examining the evidence adduced to support, refute, and qualify the hypothesis. We evaluate study methodologies and data interpretation as well as policy recommendations. Finally, we conclude that the evidence and arguments for the inequality hypothesis are wanting in many respects and that a number of influential scholars have jumped to policy implications on the basis of ideologically appealing but technically dubious findings.

2

Origins of the Inequality Hypothesis

The income inequality hypothesis originated as an ad hoc explanation for the repeated observation that income inequality (the extent to which wealth is concentrated or dispersed over a population) is associated with mortality levels. The greater the degree of inequality, the higher the mortality levels in that population.[9] Antecedents of this line of academic thinking can be traced back to at least the 1970s, when income inequality emerged on the margins of the public health literature in the form of neo-Marxist jeremiads. This direction of argumentation was particularly associated with Johns Hopkins Professor Vincente Navarro and the publication he edited, the *International Journal of Health Services*. Navarro and his colleagues maintained that the capitalist system necessarily generated both economic inequality and ill health, and that it did so in rich and poor countries alike.[10] This initial neo-Marxist thesis linking capitalism, inequality, and disease was fundamentally nonquantitative, however, and relied more on assertion and Marxist scripture than on careful data analysis to bolster its case. It would take almost two decades for some of Navarro's tenets to be tested in a more quantifiable manner by more mainstream scholars.

One of the earliest studies arguing for a causal link between health and income inequality appeared in the *British Medical Journal* in 1992.[11] In "Income Distribution and Life Expectancy," Richard Wilkinson compared nine Western industrialized countries and reported that those with less income inequality had populations with longer life expectancies. Wilkinson is easily the most vocal proponent of the so-called social production theory of health; since the appearance of his seminal article, well over two dozen research studies and commentaries confirming the income inequality hypothesis have been published.[12]

Wilkinson and other supporters of the hypothesis argue that health is one of the most sensitive indicators of the social costs of inequality. Beyond a relatively modest level of economic development, they argue, further advances in standard of living seem not to matter much, and the linear relationship between life expectancy and income breaks down.[13] This observation prompted Wilkinson to ask the following questions: How can one country "be more than twice as rich as another without being any healthier? . . . Why is life expectancy higher in countries like Greece, Japan, Iceland, and Italy than it is in richer countries like the United States or Germany? . . . What's going on?"[14]

3

Research Studies

Several lines of exploration have been pursued to answer these questions. In this section, we examine the three main types of studies conducted—aggregate data studies; individual-level analyses; and studies of human and animal social hierarchies—and analyze their implications for the income inequality hypothesis. The first type of study examines correlations between aggregate levels of health (that is, the mortality of a specified population) and income inequality. These aggregate data studies purport to offer evidence that inequality affects all members of a group, not just the poorest ones. The second type of analysis measures the effect of income inequality on health *after controlling* for the effects of individual income. These individual-level analyses ask the following question: Can the observed correlation between inequality and health be explained by the intervention of other variables, or is there truly a causal relationship between the two? The third area of exploration comprises observational studies of human social hierarchies and manipulation of animal groups. These studies, which help establish patterns of disease and health status in relation to social position, form the basis for speculation about the mechanisms by which environmental factors create stress or lead to behaviors that produce adverse health consequences.

Aggregate Data Studies

One of the earliest studies of this phenomenon was conducted in 1979 by G. B. Rodgers of the International Labour Organization, who examined income dispersion applying the Gini coefficient (a measure of income distribution) to data from fifty-six rich and poor countries in the context of three health measures: life expectancy at birth, life expectancy at age five, and the infant mortality rate (deaths in the first year of life per 1,000 live births).[15] Rodgers concluded that the "difference in average life expectancy between a relatively equalitarian and a relatively inegalitarian country is likely to be as much as five to ten years."[16] In the 1980s a handful of studies used the Gini coefficient in analyzing the relationship between health measures and found similar results.[17] Notably, Rodgers posited only a correlation, not a causal relationship, between health and income. So too did Julian Le Grand, professor of social policy at the London School of Economics. Le Grand's 1987 study found a negative association between the "absolute mean difference" in age at death and the reported share of overall income earned by the bottom quintile of the population in seventeen countries in the Organization for Economic Cooperation and Development (OECD) and in Eastern Europe. Le Grand described this finding as "intriguing," but not an indication of causality.[18]

In his 1992 study, Wilkinson suggested a causal relationship. He examined OECD countries using data from the Luxembourg Income Study and found a high correlation between life expectancy and the proportion of income earned by the bottom 70 percent of the population. Wilkinson concluded that gross national product (GNP), by itself, could not explain more than 10 percent of the variance in life expectancy and that mortality rates are not related to per-capita economic growth but rather to the scale of economic inequality in each society. The association was unaffected by adjustment made for average absolute income level and remained evident across a range of decile shares of income distribution. Subsequent to Wilkinson's report, a series of cross-national studies have demonstrated that the more even the distribution of income, the higher the life expectancy.

Ronald J. Waldmann of Columbia University complemented these findings by using another measure of inequality.[19] He examined pairs of countries in which the poor (defined as the lower 20 percent of household income distribution) had equal real incomes but where the rich (defined as the top 5 percent of the household income distribution) in one country were much wealthier than in the other. He found that the infant mortality rate was higher in the half of the pair in which the rich households were wealthier. He tested for explanations other than income, including the degree of urbanization of the households, the literacy of the mothers, and access to medical services, but found that none adequately accounted for the positive association, likely causal in his view, between the incomes of the rich and infant mortality.

In their book, *Is Inequality Bad for Our Health?* Harvard researchers Norman Daniels, Bruce Kennedy, and Ichiro Kawachi describe their cross-country analysis of per-capita gross domestic product (GDP) and life expectancy.[20] They highlight seeming paradoxes such as the fact that equally poor countries such as Cuba and Iraq do not have similar life expectancies— Cuba's reportedly exceeded that of Iraq by about seventeen years. Conversely, low GDP per capita Costa Rica and high GDP per capita United States were said to have similar life expectancies. And comparably wealthy countries with more equal income distributions, such as Sweden and Japan, had higher life expectancies (by two to five years) than the United States. The authors conclude that "the health of a population depends not just on the size of the economic pie but on how the pie is shared . . . the degree of relative deprivation within a society also matters."[21]

Numerous studies of the U.S. population have examined the association between income inequality and aggregate health measures at the state level. Below the state level, some argue, U.S. communities are too homogeneous to observe a significant association between inequality and health.[22] At that level of resolution, Daniels, Kennedy, and Kawachi found that in the United States between 1980 and 1990, states with the highest income inequality showed slower rates of improvement in average life expectancy than did states with more equitable income distributions.[23] They concluded, "The more unequal a society is in economic terms, the more unequal it is in health terms. Middle-income groups in a country with high income inequality typically do worse in terms of health than comparable or even poorer groups in a society with less income inequality."[24]

George Kaplan of the University of Michigan and his colleagues used as their measure of inequality the share of the total income earned by the bottom half of all households in each state in the United States.[25] Theoretically, if all incomes were equal, both halves of the population would account for exactly half of the aggregate income. In reality, the income share in the lower half of households ranged from 17.5 percent in Louisiana to 23.6 percent in New Hampshire. The authors found a strong correlation between this measure of inequality and death rates; the effect was present in men and women and in whites and African Americans. The study was widely credited as an important expansion of Wilkinson's work because of the range of additional variables tested. In particular, the authors found that income inequality was significantly associated with a higher incidence of age-specific mortality, low birth weight, homicide, violent crime, work disability, welfare receipt, smoking, expenditures on medical care, unemployment, and low educational attainment: all these measures worsened with increased income dispersion.

Researchers at the Harvard School of Public Health relied upon a measure of income distribution they dubbed the "Robin Hood Index."[26] It is a measure of the proportion of total income that must be redistributed from "rich" (above-mean) households to "poor" (below-mean) ones to obtain perfect equality. Using this index, the researchers found that inequality in the United States was closely linked to overall death rates within the states, as well as to higher rates of death from heart disease and cancer, homicide and infant mortality. The relationship persisted after correction for urban and rural residency, poverty rates, median income, and known health risks such as cigarette smoking. The authors predicted that if the magnitude of inequality in the United States were reduced to a level comparable to England's, this country's rate of death from heart disease would decrease by 25 percent.

While most within-country analyses focus on the United States, Yoav Ben-Shlomo, of the University of Bristol, and colleagues studied England.[27] They obtained data on the country's roughly 8,000 wards and examined the relationship between measures of deprivation and mortality before age sixty-five. They found a strong gradient in premature mortality related to deprivation (as measured by the Townsend Deprivation Index) between 1981 and 1985. The phenomenon held for male and female mortality analyzed separately. The authors concluded, "Results support the hypothesis that variation in income contributes an additional effect on mortality over the effect of deprivation alone."[28]

Individual-Level Analyses

The association between income inequality and health outcomes is not as secure as its proponents suggest. Questions remain about the extent to which statistical artifact has been mistaken for real effect. In his 1998 article "How Much of the Relation between Population Mortality and Unequal Distribution of Income Is a Statistical Artifact?" Hugh Gravelle asserts that there may be a very simple explanation for some, or all, of the reported associations between inequality of income and population health used to support the relative income hypothesis. "A positive correlation between population mortality and income inequality can arise at aggregate level even if inequality has no effect on the individual risk of mortality," he states. "Thus, we do not need the relative income hypothesis to explain the observed associations between population health and income inequality—the absolute income hypothesis will serve."[29]

International comparisons show that with increasing wealth, health improvements become smaller and smaller. Thus, the relationship between per-capita income and national health (however it is measured) should not be expected to be linear. To the contrary, as Jennifer Mellor of the College of William & Mary and Jeffrey Milyo of the University of Chicago argue, the function is one in which we would expect to see "diminishing returns" to average income—and that health levels should depend not only on average income levels but also on income distribution. This is because information on income distribution serves as a proxy for the number of persons at lower levels of income. Consequently, Mellor and Milyo conclude, aggregated ecological studies do not offer convincing evidence on this matter.[30] Harold Pollack of the University of Michigan puts it another way: "Money matters near the bottom of the distribution and may not matter at all for many outcomes when one exceeds the median. Controlling for the median income, then, any income dispersion measure is highly correlated with the percentage of the population that is under the poverty line."[31]

The influence of particular variables is significant as well. For example, when individual characteristics replace aggregate-level mortality in the analyses, and when different years are examined, the relationship between health and income inequality often disappears.[32] When the strong regional patterns in health outcome that exist across the United States are ignored, spurious associations between inequality and health may result.[33] Some, like Pollack, question the validity of one of the major econometric measures used in most analyses: "Cross-sectional regressions that use inequality measures such as Gini are virtually uninterpretable."[34] There are some glaring exceptions to the income inequality pattern. In Denmark, for example, where per-capita income is similar to that of the United States but where income dispersion is lower, life expectancy is below that of the United States. Thus the important but unanswered question of metric remains: Is reported annual dispersion of a society's income the most appropriate index for describing inequality in that population?[35]

Questions of Causation. Milyo and Mellor have questioned whether the correlation between inequality and health is spurious, not causal. There are three possible interpretations of a correlation between variables A and B. It is possible that A causes B, that B causes A, or that A and B are independent of each other but both are related to a third variable. Taking into account the well-established relationship between health and material well-being and social status, Milyo and Mellor point out obvious advantages that come with wealth: well-off people can afford better health insurance and higher quality care; demand better work environments; live in less polluted and less crime-ridden neighborhoods; and afford safer cars. In this way, being richer can make one healthier. Yet consider the reverse dynamic: being healthy can also make one better off. Poor physical or mental health can influence an individual's ability to work or to work long hours, thus limiting his income. This is known as the "healthy worker effect." What follows could lead to further health impairment because the worker has less money with which to purchase health-enhancing goods and protections. The cumulative wear and tear on such individuals, coupled with whatever psychic stress they experience as a result of deprivation of social status, may be considerable.

Additionally, so-called third factors can account for the habits and limited opportunities that often lead to poorer health. Sedentary lifestyle, obesity, high-fat diets, aversion to medical care, and risky behavior, which typically underlie many of the differences in health status between the less wealthy and the better off, may well be the product of educational level. Better-informed people know about the importance of exercise, screening tests for cancer, and a diet that includes fruits and vegetables. They are more confident when interacting with physicians and better at negotiating bureaucracies (for example, HMOs). Personal characteristics that tend to be associated with greater life success, such as prudence, perseverance, and ability to delay gratification, are also likely predictors of good health or competence in managing illness. Indeed, the substantial association of health with certain measures of human capital suggests that income inequality itself may not have a direct effect on mortality. The association more likely reflects the effects of other factors—education in particular—that are also related to mortality. Andreas Muller of the University of Arkansas tested whether the relationship between income inequality and mortality in the United States is a consequence of different levels of formal education.[36] He conducted state-by-state analyses of age-adjusted mortality from all causes and three independent variables: the Gini coefficient on income in 1989 and 1990, per-capita income from those years, and the percentage of people older than eighteen who did not complete high school.

An income inequality effect was found, but it disappeared when the percentage of people without a high school diploma was added to the regression analysis. Muller concluded that the lack of a high school education accounts for the income inequality effect and is a powerful predictor of mortality variation across states. He writes, "The physical and social conditions associated with low levels of education may be sufficient for interpretation of the relationship between income inequality and mortality."[37] These conditions likely include the risk of occupational injury, the inability to attain protective goods and services (for example, a safe car, health care), and cigarette smoking.

In another analysis, RAND researchers examined specific chronic physical and mental conditions and found that the relationship between income inequality and health disappeared.[38] The researchers used 1997–1998 data from sixty metropolitan areas in the United States, as well as self-reports of specific diagnoses (for example, arthritis, asthma, low back pain, depression) gathered by telephone survey. The association between Gini coefficient for each of the sixty areas and between individual income data and the prevalence of each medical disorder was tested. Age, sex, race, and size of family were taken into account. The authors found that the prevalence of most conditions decreased continuously across most of the income ranges. The prevalence of chronic conditions did not vary with the extent of income dispersion across the sixty areas. In particular, the highest prevalence for every condition occurred in one of the two poorest fifths of an area's population as stratified by income.

James S. House of the University of Michigan has remarked on his colleagues' tendency to place "excessive focus" on income inequality as a health determinant.[39] He finds that almost all behavioral, environmental, psychological, and social risk factors for health become more prevalent with decreasing income and reduction in other forms of socioeconomic status and resources such as education or occupation. These conditions of life, House says, along with remaining inequalities in medical care, can largely explain why income is so strongly linked to health "without recourse to notions of relative deprivation, lack of social trust or cohesion."[40]

Ecological Fallacy. From a methodological standpoint, most quantitative research purporting to support the inequality thesis is potentially compromised by a problem statisticians designate as "ecological bias." Ecological bias arises when "ecological correlations"—that is to say, correlations witnessed in aggregated data—differ from the underlying correlations that would be observed if one were examining individual data.

Examples of confounding "ecological correlations" abound in the social sciences. One particularly famous case is highlighted in sociologist W. S. Robinson's classic 1950 study of ecological bias. In this study, Robinson points out that U.S. Census Bureau data demonstrated a clear negative correlation between the proportion of a state's population that was foreign-born and the state's illiteracy rate—that is, the higher a state's foreign-born population, the lower its illiteracy rate. From that correlation, one might well infer that the foreign-born population in America was more literate than the native-born population—but that inference would be wrong. Literacy levels for the foreign-born population were actually *lower* than for U.S.-born citizens, but these immigrants were more likely to be concentrated in states where the native population's literacy rate was high. At the state level, intervening ecological biases distorted and indeed entirely misrepresented the true correspondence between literacy and nativity that would have been seen by looking directly at characteristics evident in individuals themselves. As Robinson warned over half a century ago, ecological correlations cannot "validly be used as a substitute for individual correlations":

> While it is theoretically possible for the two to be equal, the conditions under which this can happen are far removed from those encountered in data. From a practical

Figure 1: Health vs. Wealth Internationally: Per-Capita GDP vs. Life Expectancy at Birth, 1990

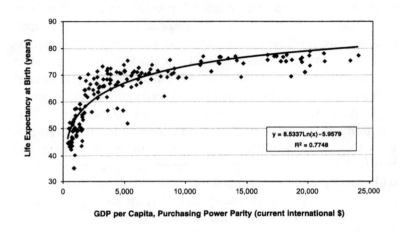

GDP per Capita, Purchasing Power Parity (current international $)

SOURCE: International Bank for Reconstruction and Development, *World Development Indicators 2001* (Washington, D.C.: World Bank, 2001), CD-ROM.

NOTE: Ln = Natural logarithm.

standpoint, therefore, the only reasonable assumption is that an ecological correlation is almost certainly not equal to its corresponding individual correlation.[41]

Ecological bias is a particular risk in studies of the inequality thesis for a very simple reason: the relationship between income and mortality is highly unlikely to be linear. In general, an individual's health will not be doubled by a doubling of income—and multiplying his or her income by a factor of ten will not correspondingly reduce mortality odds or health risks by an order of magnitude. To the contrary, in almost all populations the relationship between income and mortality seems to be curvilinear, that is, additional increments in income correspond to further improvements—albeit steadily diminishing improvements.

Figure 1 illustrates the general shape of the correspondence between income and mortality within populations. This figure plots life expectancy against per-capita GNP for 1990 in the 159 countries for which the World Bank's database offered estimates. As figure 1 indicates, this international relationship conforms fairly closely to a "log-linear" pattern, that is, a *proportional* increase in per-capita income corresponds with a *constant absolute* increase in life expectancy. In the particular case of figure 1, the shape of the curve is such that a doubling of a population's per-capita income is associated with an increase of about six years in a population's life expectancy.

Consider what this curvilinear correspondence between income and mortality means for aggregated data—and for measurements to test the inequality hypothesis. Even if increased income dispersion has no negative impact whatever upon health, the society with the higher level of income inequality will, all things being equal, appear to have an "unexpectedly" short life expectancy.

A simple hypothetical example illustrates the problem (see table 1). Suppose we invent a country called "Equalia," with a population of 100,000. Every person in Equalia earns the national median income of $50,000 a year, and every person lives exactly seventy-five years. In this country, then, life expectancy is seventy-five, average per-capita income is $50,000, and the Gini coefficient of income inequality is exactly zero (on a possible scale of zero to 100 percent).

Now suppose an invented individual—call him "Bill Gates"—suddenly moves to Equalia. Bill's income is $5 billion a year, and his life expectancy (thanks in part to the superb medical treatment he is able to afford) is exactly one hundred. Suppose further that Bill's immigration leaves everyone else's income and health totally unaffected.

What will aggregated data show? Before Bill came to Equalia, life expectancy was seventy-five; after he moved in, it was ever so slightly above seventy-five. Before he moved in, average income per household was $50,000; after he arrived, average income was virtually twice as high—essentially, $100,000 per household. And whereas the Gini coefficient for Equalia's income distribution was zero before Bill's arrival, post-Bill Equalia would have a Gini coefficient of nearly 50 (half of the country's income would be in Bill's hands, and the rest would be evenly distributed among everyone else).

Table 1: "Equalia" Before and After the Arrival of "Bill Gates"—An Illustrative Exercise

"Equalia" Before "Bill Gates" Arrives

Population	100,000 people
Life Expectancy	each person lives exactly 75 years
Per-Capita Income	exactly $50,000 per year
Total Wage Fund	$5 billion per year
Gini Coefficient	0.0

"Bill Gates"

Population	1 person
Life Expectancy	exactly 100 years
Income	exactly $5 billion per year

"Equalia" After "Bill Gates" Arrives

Population	100,001 people
Life Expectancy	approximately 75.0 (75.001)
Per-Capita Income	approximately $100,000 ($99,999)
Total Wage Fund	$10 billion per year
Gini Coefficient	approximately 50.0

Source: Authors' calculations.

By the sort of analysis the inequality thesis school favors, post-Bill Equalia would be placed on a scatter plot along with other populations and compared in terms of mortality (or life expectancy), income, and income distribution measures. Of course, life expectancy in the country would be almost identical before and after Bill's move. But post-Bill Equalia's income level would be far higher than that of pre-Bill Equalia, and the country's income distribution would be more uneven. The correspondence between life expectancy and income in post-Bill Equalia would look much less favorable than in pre-Bill Equalia—indeed, if we used the relationships in figure 1 as a benchmark, post-Bill Equalia might be seen as "suffering" from a national life expectancy fully six years lower than might have been expected on the basis of its income level alone. Further use of regression analysis could produce results that would demonstrate that income inequality in post-Bill Equalia had cost the nation years of lost life expectancy (against levels otherwise predicted). Yet in our hypothetical example, not a single household in Equalia had its health or income affected by Bill's entry into the country. The adverse relationship between inequality and health suggested by nation-level data in post-Bill Equalia is entirely spurious—a consequence of ecological bias, pure and simple.

It is not only in hypothetical examples that "ecological correlation" may misrepresent the true correspondence between health risks and economic stratification. Ecological fallacy may also undermine conclusions from previous studies supporting the income inequality hypothesis. Thus, it is important to control for confounding at the individual level. To that end, Kevin Fiscella and Peter Franks of the University of Rochester School of Medicine and Dentistry examined whether the relationship between income inequality and mortality observed at the population level may simply represent inadequately measured rates of income differences at the individual level.[42]

Fiscella and Franks used demographic and mortality data from 1971 and 1987 from the first National Health and Nutrition Examination Survey and related follow-up surveys. Additional data were obtained from follow-up interview surveys, medical records from healthcare institutions, and all death certificates. To measure income inequality, the researchers used an index that estimates the proportion of total income earned by the poorer half of the population in an area. The authors found that aggregated data replicated earlier findings that supported the income inequality hypothesis; after they adjusted for individual household income, however, no significant relation between income inequality and mortality was evident. "Our findings imply that income, as a measure of access to resources, and not relative inequality, better explains the relation between income and mortality."[43]

Merete Osler and colleagues at the University of Copenhagen also sought to disentangle the effects of income on mortality at the aggregate level from those on the individual level. Their study was the first to examine whether area-based measures of income inequality predict all-cause mortality after adjustment for individual income and risk factors in a society outside the United States.[44] From the Danish national statistical agency, they obtained registers of income statistics for all residents of Denmark over age fifteen. Other data came from population studies, self-administered questionnaires, and health examinations, which yielded information on smoking, alcohol consumption, physical activity, and education. For each of the 149 parishes under study, the authors measured income inequality using the median parish income as a proportion of the total household gross income earned by the poorer half of households in the parish.

The authors found no association between income inequality at the parish level and all-cause mortality after adjustment for individual income. They did, however, confirm the well-established inverse relation between individual income and mortality. The authors speculate that Denmark's welfare system may "even out" the effect of area inequality. It is also possible that such a small geographical area is too low a level of resolution for the dynamics predicted by Kawachi and colleagues to operate. For example, perhaps individuals feel relatively deprived when they perceive themselves as part of a larger social landscape. Or possibly underinvestment in social services and public resources is less a problem in smaller areas because poorer residents of such areas may feel more like neighbors than they would in a larger setting.

Other Perspectives. Few studies explicitly test whether inequality has a more pronounced effect on the health of the poor. In those that do, the results are mixed at best. Ellen Meara of Harvard University examined the relationship between various measures of household income inequality on infant mortality and low birth weight.[45] She estimated the effects of inequality with and without state-specific effects—that is to say, taking into account the possibility that particular states might have especially good, or poor, health outcomes due to some special intrinsic circumstance. After

controlling for household income and other maternal characteristics, Meara found no significant correlation between
income inequality and adverse birth outcomes among poorer
women.

Mellor and Milyo also explicitly examined whether inequality
has a particularly strong effect on poorer individuals. They controlled for the possibility that particular regions of the country
might have characteristically better or worse health than other
regions—possibly due to factors such as local dietary or behavioral habits that could be spuriously correlated with income
inequality—and explored whether the relationship between
health and income inequality is robust across geographical units.
They found that statistical association between income inequality
and health outcomes is greatly attenuated once controls are added
for individual income. In fact, when Mellor and Milyo controlled
for variables such as education and race, they found a weak
inverse relationship—that is, the more dispersed a state's income,
the less healthy the individuals.[46]

Little research is explicitly devoted to testing the theory that
perception of relative deprivation leads to illness or foreshortened
lifespan. Angus Deaton and Christina Paxson of Princeton
University attempted to do this by measuring inequality within
birth cohorts rather than across geographical regions.[47] The
authors reasoned that people may be more likely to appraise their
social status differently if they compare themselves to others at the
same stage of life rather than with their neighbors. They found no
robust association between inequality and mortality when
inequality is measured within birth cohort; in fact, in some spec-
ifications, the association was the opposite of what the income
inequality hypothesis would predict.

Causal Mechanisms. In much of the inequality thesis literature
to date, the presumed intermediate variable through which economic inequality takes its toll on health is said to be "social capital." The links in this chain of reasoning are by no means as sturdy
as some proponents of the thesis seem to believe.

Social capital (a measure of civic cohesion) is a fairly new the-oretical construct; it did not enter general academic parlance until after James Coleman's 1988 exposition on its role in "human cap-ital" formation.[48] As sociologist Pamela Paxton has observed, "The term 'social capital' has been used in many recent articles but in vastly different ways."[49] Measuring social capital is correspond-ingly problematic: there is no self-evident "best" measure for social capital, and alternative indexes can produce contrasting or even contradictory readings for a given society.[50]

The notion that a society's health profile might be affected by its endowment and/or distribution of social capital is, on its face, entirely plausible. Although work in this area is still exploratory, some initial studies have suggested that social capital can be shown to exert an independent influence on individual health in given settings.[51]

Even if there proves to be a robust correspondence between health and social capital, however, it does not necessarily follow that economic inequality per se has a direct bearing on health prospects. If that were true, there would have to be a causal relationship between inequality and social capital formation, but available evidence suggests that even the statistical association between economic inequality and social capital is quite tenuous.

This dubious relationship is evident in table 2, which compares estimates of economic inequality for countries and areas designated as "high trust" and "low trust" societies by Francis Fukuyama in his seminal study on social capital.[52] In Fukuyama's estimate, Germany, Japan, and the United States are countries with high lev-els of social capital, while France, Italy, Hong Kong, and Taiwan are settings where the endowment of social capital is noticeably lower. But as official economic statistics illustrate, no obvious correspon-dence exists between income inequality and social trust among Fukuyama's exemplars. It is true that economic inequality (as meas-ured by the Gini coefficient) is on average somewhat higher in the "low trust" than the "high trust" societies identified (36 versus 32, respectively). But income inequality would also seem to be greater in "high trust" Germany than in "low trust" Italy (30 versus 27).

Table 2: Reported Differences in Income Distribution in
         Countries and Locales Designated as "High Trust"
         and "Low Trust" in Fukuyama (1995)

"High Trust"	
Country/Locale	Gini Coefficient
Germany (1994)	30.0
Japan (1993)	24.9
United States (1997)	40.8

"Low Trust"	
Country/Locale	Gini Coefficient
Hong Kong (1996)	52.2
Italy (1995)	27.3
France (1995)	32.7
Taiwan (1995)	32.5

SOURCE: Francis Fukuyama, *Trust: The Social Virtues and the Creation of Prosperity* (New York: Free Press, 1995); World Bank, *World Development Report 2003* (New York: Oxford University Press, 2003); Republic of China Directorate-General of Budgeting, Accounting, and Statistics; data available electronically at http://www.gio.gov.tw/info/taiwan-story/economy/edown/table/table-11.htm.

Income distribution would appear to be distinctly more skewed in "high trust" America (with a Gini coefficient of about 41) than in either "low trust" France or "low trust" Taiwan (both of which are reported to have Gini coefficients of about 33). And within the "low trust" group, Italy's measured level of income inequality is barely half that of Hong Kong (27 versus 52). Indeed, according to World Bank data, outside of Scandinavia and the former Soviet bloc, no country in the world today reports a more even distribution of national income than does "low trust" Italy.[53]

If the international relationship between inequality and social capital is questionable, the relationship within particular countries over time is hardly much stronger. The United States is a case in point. According to U.S. Census Bureau data, America's Gini coefficient for family income distribution in the post–World War II period has a sort of "U" shape, with measured inequality gradually declining from the late 1940s through the late 1960s and rising gradually from the late 1960s to the present day.[54] Those attempting to quantify "social capital" disagree about long-term trends for post-war America: some see a gradual decline; others, a decline from the 1970s onward; and still others, an effective long-term stasis.[55] None of these specialists, however, has proposed that trends in U.S. social capital have followed the sort of parabolic path necessary to establish a robust statistical association with long-term trends in American income inequality.

Given the current weak empirical foundations for any argument linking inequality and social capital, the hypothetical mechanism by which inequality would have an impact on health would seem to remain just that—merely hypothetical.

Replicability of Results. The essence of the scientific method is to frame and operationalize a hypothesis whose predictions comport with observable results in a consistent manner. If the hypothesis is valid and testable, its result should be generally reproducible, rather than unique to a particular experimental attempt. Some of the important studies adduced in support of the inequality hypothesis, however, appear to be difficult to replicate with different but analogous sets of data.

Waldmann's influential 1992 study on international infant mortality rates and economic inequality is a case in point. Although Waldmann himself has not been an exponent of the inequality thesis, his econometric analysis—which found that "infant mortality is higher when the income of the rich is higher"[56]—has become staple fare for those who argue that inequality per se has adverse effects on public health. Waldmann wrote that "infant mortality appears to be positively related to the incomes of the rich (the upper 5 percent of the income distribution) when the incomes of the poor (the lowest 20 percent) are equalized among countries." He took this result to be so robust that he described it as a "striking empirical regularity."[57]

If this is indeed a striking empirical regularity, it would be reasonable to expect a similar result using more recent data. In his 1992 *Quarterly Journal of Economics* study, Waldmann drew on

World Bank per-capita income and income distribution data from the 1960s and 1970s for a sample of fifty-seven countries, forty-one of which he categorized as "developing countries." Today we can use larger and more recent World Bank data. The World Bank now provides estimates of income distribution in the mid-1990s for 117 countries, more than 90 of which would be classified as developing countries under Waldmann's typology. We thought it would be interesting to repeat Waldmann's analysis on these new data, using the same regression equations that generated his striking and thought-provoking conclusions. The results of that analysis are shown in tables 3 and 4.

Waldmann examined the international relationship between infant mortality and economic inequality through four initial regressions: two for all countries in his data sample and two for developing countries alone. The first set of equations attempted to predict infant mortality on the basis of the average per-capita income of the lowest 20 percent of the population, the average per-capita income of the middle 70 percent of the population, and the share of income accruing to the wealthiest 5 percent of the population. The second set of equations omitted the middle 70 percent, and tried to predict infant mortality rates solely on the basis of the poorest fifth's income level and the richest 5 percent's income share. (Waldmann also added a dummy variable for the 1970s to check whether the relationship between infant mortality and these other factors had changed between the 1960s and the 1970s.) We were able to gather estimates for the share of income accruing to the poorest 20 percent, the middle 70 percent, and the richest 10 percent of the population for the countries in our sample—indicators not identical to Waldmann's but close nonetheless. (Unlike Waldmann, we did not need to use a dummy variable for different decades because our data set pertained to a single time period, the mid-1990s.)

As table 3 indicates, the "striking empirical regularity" that Waldmann found in 1992 is not at all evident in international data from the mid-1990s. For the sample of all countries— rich and poor—recent data affirm Waldmann's finding of a strong

Table 3: Revisiting Waldmann (1992): Rerunning Regressions on the International Relationship Between Economic Inequality and Infant Mortality with an Updated and Enlarged Data Set

	Dependent Variable: Ln^1 (Infant Mortality Rate)			
	Waldmann All	Eberstadt-Satel All	Waldmann Developing	Eberstadt-Satel Developing
N	57	117	41	89
R^2	0.79	0.87	0.56	0.73
Constant	11.92 (13.2)	9.33 (22.8)	11.41 (7.7)	9.47 (18.9)
1970 Variable	0.06 (0.44)	N/A	–0.05 (–0.25)	N/A
Ln (Poor Income)	0.07 (0.45)	0.05 (0.30)	0.01 (0.04)	0.07 (0.19)
Ln (Middle Income)	–0.8 (–5.57)	–0.86 (–5.12)	–0.69 (–3.18)	–0.89 (–4.49)
Rich Share	2.48 (2.82)	0.02 (2.18)	2.43 (2.32)	0.02 (1.80)

SOURCE: Robert J. Waldmann, "Income Distribution and Infant Mortality," *Quarterly Journal of Economics* 107, no. 4 (November 1992): 1287; International Bank for Reconstruction and Development, *World Development Indicators 2001* (Washington, D.C.: World Bank, 2001), CD-ROM.

NOTE: Numbers in parentheses are t-statistics; "Developing" in Eberstadt-Satel is total set minus OECD members.

(1) Ln = Natural logarithm.

and statistically significant relationship between infant mortality and the per-capita income levels of the middle income grouping (hardly a surprising result, insofar as this middle group accounts for the overwhelming majority of each country's population, and also presumably the greatest share of every country's births and infant deaths). But where Waldmann uncovered a powerful and significant positive relationship between infant mortality and the share of income accruing to the top income grouping, our analysis finds a negligible association: the absolute value of the coefficient that we calculate is less than one hundredth the size of Waldmann's. The results of the regressions for the developing countries by themselves are even less persuasive. Once again, our coefficient relating the income share of the rich to infant mortality rates is one hundred times smaller than Waldmann's. This time, our calculated coefficient is not statistically significant at the 5 percent confidence level—that is to say, with the confidence intervals commonly held out for findings, we cannot tell whether the sign on this variable is positive or negative!

Results appear even more incongruent in table 4. When just the income level of the poor and the income share of the rich are used to predict infant mortality, Waldmann found a strong and positive association between inequality (so measured) and the infant mortality rate. But in the mid-1990s, using a much larger data set, that relationship is weak—and the coefficient is negative. This is true for a sample including both rich and poor countries, and for developing countries by themselves. Given the very low level of statistical significance for these rerun coefficients, we can have no confidence that the value of these coefficients differs from zero. Based on our data samples and the regressions in table 4, there is no indication whatsoever that the share of total income going to the wealthy has any influence whatever on a country's infant mortality rate.

Far from being a striking empirical regularity, the purported perverse association between international inequality and infant mortality rates appears to be highly conditional. More specifically, it appears to be contingent upon the data set selected to demonstrate it. Anomalous results are sometimes just that—anomalous results. This is a fact worth remembering in evaluating all quantitative social research, not simply studies bearing on the inequality hypothesis.

Social scientists commonly use a "P-value" of 5 percent to test the statistical significance of findings—that is, the results will be accepted only if there is no more than a 5 percent probability that they could have been generated by chance. But using a 5 percent P-value also means that, on average, every twentieth totally random result will be accepted as real and statistically meaningful.

Table 4: Revisiting Waldmann (1992), continued: Rerunning Regressions on the International Relationship Between Economic Inequality and Infant Mortality with an Updated and Enlarged Data Set

	Dependent Variable: Ln[1] (Infant Mortality Rate)			
	Waldmann All	Eberstadt-Satel All	Waldmann Developing	Eberstadt-Satel Developing
N	57	117	41	89
R^2	0.66	0.83	0.44	0.68
Constant	9.48 (9.55)	9.26 (20.5)	8.42 (6.58)	9.1 (16.6)
Ln (Poor Income)	−0.66 (−6.95)	−0.79 (−19.9)	−0.50 (−3.54)	−0.75 (−13.0)
Rich Share	1.09 (1.03)	−0.01 (−1.80)	1.16 (1.07)	−0.01 (−1.88)

SOURCE: Robert J. Waldmann, "Income Distribution and Infant Mortality," *Quarterly Journal of Economics* 107, no. 4 (November 1992): 1287; International Bank for Reconstruction and Development, *World Development Indicators 2001* (Washington, D.C.: World Bank, 2001), CD-ROM.

NOTE: Numbers in parentheses are t-statistics; "Developing" in Eberstadt-Satel is total set minus OECD members.

(1) Ln = Natural logarithm.

The danger of accepting as genuine what are in truth artifacts becomes steadily greater with the number of regressions and statistical data tests that a social scientist happens to run (a fact that should be borne in mind by researchers striving to find substantiation for their own hypotheses).

Studies of Health in Human and Animal Social Hierarchies

The inequality hypothesis has generated speculation about mechanisms through which economic arrangements translate into health effects. Scholars have proposed two general pathways by which the relative deprivation intrinsic to hierarchy can lead to higher levels of infant mortality and infirmity and to shorter life expectancy. The first pathway is through the stress of feeling isolated, subjugated, disenfranchised, hopelessness, abandoned. The second is through material disadvantage that includes, among other things, inferior access to health care. Researchers John Lynch and George Kaplan of the University of Michigan claim that lower levels of social cohesion will result in a lower level of social investment in the poorer members of society; they speculate about the characteristics of a society that "tolerates," in their words, its own stratification.[58]

Social Position. Wilkinson points to a pattern in which the health of a society appears strongly affected by the social position of its members and by their relative rather than absolute income levels. He argues that people judge their lot in life by comparing their own situation with that of others. The greater the difference between the upper and lower rungs of the socioeconomic ladder, the more acutely aware those at the bottom become of those at the top. Recognition of this disparity, Wilkinson says, engenders psychological stress that leads to physical illness such as cardiovascular disease. Stress could also cause depression or irritability, which, he speculates, makes people more prone to violence or accidents.

Social position theorists draw upon the solid experimental literature about time-limited stress as a mediator of physiological responses (immune, cardiovascular, nervous system) to environmental change.[59] And examples abound. In the world of primates, subordinate female baboons have been diagnosed with impaired ovarian function, lower sex steroid concentrations, and more arterial sclerosis than their higher-ranking counterparts. The assumption that low-ranking animals are stressed is based on the observation that they are more often the targets of aggression, are hypervigilant, spend more time by themselves, have suppressed reproductive function, and secrete higher-than-normal levels of cortisol (a stress hormone).[60] In the human universe, numerous studies have documented an association between emotional state, especially anger and hostility, and cardiovascular disease.[61]

In an exhaustive book on the topic, *Anger, Hostility, and the Heart,* psychologist Aron W. Siegman classifies two types of anger: withheld anger (also called repressed anger) and expressed anger. Siegman documents scores of studies showing a relationship between both kinds of anger and increased blood pressure, stronger contractility of the heart (sometimes experienced as palpitations), and irregular heartbeats.[62] The consensus among scientists is that chronic, low-grade stress is not good for one's health. The precise mechanism by which "control-of-destiny" stress might translate into physical damage such as sustained hypertension, heart attack, or heart failure is not known, but intriguing data and plausible theories abound.[63] Perhaps repeated frustration-induced surges in blood pressure cause trauma to the inside of blood vessels. Or perhaps stress disrupts the normal cardiac rhythm, produces a blood vessel spasm, or even leads to smoking, which in turn has its own detrimental effects on blood pressure.[64] Hormonal, neural, and immunologic changes are also probably involved in regulating the cardiovascular system.

S. Leonard Syme of Berkeley's School of Public Health was one of the first to describe the control-of-destiny theory when he examined the landmark Whitehall studies performed by researchers at University College in London.[65] The studies examined workers in the five grades of the British Civil Service, all of whom have access to nationalized health care. The researchers, led by Michael Marmot of the University of London, were not surprised that the civil servants in the lowest grade suffered heart disease at about three times the rate of administrators in the highest, or fifth, stratum, even after controlling for obvious health risks like smoking. They were puzzled, however, to find that even highly paid professionals in the fourth grade suffered twice as much cardiovascular disease as top-ranking administrators.[66] What appeared to explain this finding was the fact that these workers had little control of destiny; their jobs were fraught with responsibility, but they could exercise little authority. Marmot's practical suggestion was that employers create ways for workers to have more latitude and to break the monotony of their tasks.[67]

Another term for the "low control of destiny" phenomenon, developed independently by the psychologist Martin P. Seligman in his work with animals, is "learned helplessness"—that is, a posture of defeat and resignation, often accompanied by physical symptoms, that follows repeated failed attempts by the animal to change its environment.[68] Eventually the animal "learns" to adopt a helpless, passive stance because there is little it can do to influence events. People, too, can become passive when they feel unable to control their lives.

Social Cohesion and Social Capital. Numerous epidemiological studies have shown that people who are socially isolated die at two to three times the rate of well-connected individuals.[69] But what about entire, socially isolated communities? If populations are not well integrated socially, as reflected in a hierarchical structure that highlights real or perceived differences in interests across individuals, what effect might this have on the health of the group?

Kawachi and his colleagues at Harvard were among the first to address this question. They conducted a cross-sectional study of thirty-nine states in which they examined the relationship between social capital and mortality.[70] The aim was to estimate state variations in group membership and levels of trust. They quantified social capital by considering the per-capita number of groups and associations to which residents of each state belonged. They also weighted responses to several items on the General Social Survey conducted by the National Opinion Research Center. The first survey item was a measure of "perceived lack of fairness": "Do you think most people would try to take advantage of you if they had the chance, or would they try to be fair?" The second item was about "social mistrust": "Generally speaking, would you say that most people can be trusted or that you can't be too careful in dealing with people?" So was the third: "Would you say that most of the time people try to be helpful, or are they mostly looking out for themselves?" For each state, the authors calculated the percentage of respondents who agreed with the first part of each statement and found an association between social capital and mortality. According to the authors, "A major finding of this study is that the size of the gap between the rich and the poor is powerfully and negatively related to level of investment in social capital."[71] The authors acknowledge that their model did not consider the full range of factors that might influence income inequality and social capital. They also recognize the inability to discern the direction of causality, noting that the issue could be clarified by analyzing long-term trends in social capital and mortality.

Daniels, Kennedy, and Kawachi propose that income inequality affects health by inhibiting the formation of social capital, which in turn undermines civil society. It erodes social cohesion as indicated by higher levels of measured social mistrust and reduced participation in civic organizations. Lack of social cohesion, they argue, leads to a decline in engagement in activities and institutions such as voting, serving in local government, or volunteering for political campaigns. Low levels of engagement, in turn, undermine the responsiveness of government to addressing the needs of the worse off. The authors conclude, "States with the highest income inequality, and thus the lowest levels of social capital and political participation, are less likely to invest in human capital and provide far less generous safety nets."[72] A dearth of social capital, which makes people feel vulnerable and isolated, could lead to depression and, in turn, to illness, poor health habits, or risk-taking behavior. (After all, if one believes that he is a less-valued member of society, he will be less invested in his own well-being.)

Socioeconomics Gets into the Body. Communal animals provide insight into the behavioral and physiological concomitants of social position. Baboons and monkeys in the wild and in captivity display marked differences from their troop mates depending upon their status. Behaviorally, their superiors constantly face down subordinates of both sexes. The lower-ranking animals tend to be more fearful and vigilant and less engaged in the social events around them; they receive less grooming and playful attention from others. Physiologically, subordinates have higher circulating cortisol, greater resistance to insulin (a mechanism for keeping energy-giving glucose in circulation), and increased levels of fibrinogen (a clotting protein protective in bloody encounters).[73] In short, subordinates appear to be in a state of constant alertness. In this so-called flight-or-fight mode, their bodies are mobilizing resources for a speedy getaway or, if cornered, combat. This readiness leaves less energy available for maintenance activities like tissue repair and growth.

Bruce McEwen of Rockefeller University identified competitive interactions between animals of the same species as among the most powerful stressors social animals encounter. These seemingly mundane, grinding insults of daily life—not the dramatic conflicts between animals—produce the most stress. McEwen has popularized the term "allostatic load" to describe the many events of everyday life that cause wear and tear on physiological systems.[74] Under sustained conditions of high load, animals are more likely to develop atherosclerotic deposits in major arteries and gastric ulcers. They are more likely to succumb to infections, cancer, and stroke. Subordinates also have more parasites, fewer chances to mate, and shorter life spans than their superiors. Female monkeys in a subordinate position have poorer ovarian function, fewer menstrual cycles, and lower concentrations of sex hormones.[75]

If rank plays a significant role in shaping an animal's physiological profile, could subordinate animals be made healthier by moving them to the top tier? Carol A. Shively and Thomas B. Clarkson at Bowman Gray School of Medicine altered social status in a group of female macaque monkeys—subordinates became dominant and dominants became subordinate—and compared them with a similar group in which animals' status remained the same. Both groups were fed an atherogenic diet. After two years, all animals that changed social positions, irrespective of status change, suffered more rapid progression of atherosclerosis than their counterparts in the unperturbed control group.[76]

Specifically, the newly dominant monkeys had 44 percent more atherosclerosis than their counterparts who were not displaced, and the dethroned dominants showed an increase of 500 percent relative to their counterparts. In another study, however, Shively found that ovarian function in the subordinates-turned-dominant greatly improved.[77] As Shively concludes, "The manipulation of social status may have deleteriously altered a complex interaction between individuals and their psychosocial environment."[78]

Similarly, biological anthropologist Jay R. Kaplan and colleagues at Wake Forest University School of Medicine manipulated the social arrangements of male monkeys by moving them at monthly intervals and inserting them into an established group.[79] By circulating the animals on a regular basis, the researchers modeled the kind of social instability that is typically experienced by macaque monkeys in the wild. In the presence of the newcomer, the established dominant male was forced to reassert his social position; though most dominants managed to retain their position, the costs of doing so were high. Specifically, the dominant animals that were forced to reassert themselves after being challenged by newcomers developed roughly twice the coronary atherosclerosis as dominant animals that remained unchallenged in a stable environment.[80]

The implications of these dynamic studies are very different from those of static analyses. The latter have been interpreted to mean that hierarchy itself wholly or largely causes the physiological stigmata of stress and poorer health status of lower-ranking animals and humans. Accordingly, the healthiest society would also be the least competitive and most egalitarian. It is important to note that McEwen's model of allostatic load regards environmental impact (for example, hierarchical forces) as only one of several determinants of stress. Other factors, such as genetic traits, individual habits (for example, diet), and developmental experiences (for example, maternal deprivation), which can in turn influence physiological reactivity, also contribute to physiological wear and tear. (And in humans, the very perception of a situation as threatening plays a significant role in the intensity of a stress response.) The influence of these other variables suggests, therefore, that social placement is not randomly assigned.

In fact, dominant animals attain their rank in part because they are predisposed to be there.[81] At the very least, two attributes play a role: nepotism, wherein high-ranking members have high-ranking offspring; and "merit" (for example, brawn, skillful use of aggression, and appeasement). To be sure, the dynamics of social interaction exert an influence on the animal's psychological and somatic well-being, but intrinsic factors play a determining role as well. Thus, it is not surprising that when predetermined social arrangements are disrupted in the laboratory, the reconfigurations do not produce overall health for the group.

In sum, deliberate reorganization of social arrangements (perhaps the animal equivalent of social engineering) appears to cause more problems than it solves. The ultimate social experiment—devising an "equalized" group—remains a thought experiment since it would be impossible to obliterate gradients among animals hard-wired to sort themselves out. It is true that social forces between monkeys do not apply readily to human dynamics; yet there may be a lesson to draw about the value of social buffers. A major virtue of rank is that it affords more buffers (better food, more protection, and so on) against the ravages of stress. To the extent that the sheer stress of being subordinate has physiological ramifications, it might be wise to emphasize personal and policy interventions that reduce the psychological implications of subordination in the workplace and even in society at large. These interventions include an emphasis on autonomy and control in the work environment, the promise of upward mobility, better habits (of diet, exercise, and so on), opportunities for tension release (vacation time, entertainment), and secure emotional attachments to family and community (admittedly a difficult phenomenon for politicians and employers to shape).

4

Conclusion

This brief review of the controversy surrounding the inequality hypothesis has examined the claims of proponents of that hypothesis, the evidence adduced for the case, and the methodologies underlying the arguments used to support the hypothesis.

In our short exploration of this increasingly influential school of thought within the public health literature, some important and intriguing questions relating to the inequality hypothesis perforce could not be addressed. One pressing question, however, must not be ignored: How did it happen that a notion with such questionable empirical documentation and such a limited relationship to the testable proposition has come to acquire so much respect within the academy and so much authority in policy circles?

As we have seen, the phenomenon surely cannot be explained simply in terms of the quantitative persuasiveness of studies of the inequality hypothesis. To the contrary, the ambitious intellectual claims of this school of thinking have been undergirded by research that has all too often relied upon limited or unrepresentative data sets, hazily expounded causality, elementary econometric fallacies, and results that cannot be replicated.

Thus the widespread popularity of the inequality hypothesis must be explained in other, nonempirical terms. We would suggest that there is a profound, almost elemental, appeal to the basic premises of the hypothesis, and, most especially, to its implicit practical corollary—namely, that by restructuring society and reducing inequality, we can promise to improve the health chances and life prospects for all. This elemental theme, however, is hardly new to social or political discourse. In an important sense, the theme is as old as the concept of modernity itself. In one form or another, versions of the same romantic, utopian call have been heard ever since writers began to imagine that we could improve humanity by purposely refashioning the sort of society that human beings inhabited. Like the Marxist and neo-Marxist ideologies with which it shares parentage, the inequality hypothesis is best understood as a creed or faith, rather than an intellectual conjecture that may be embraced or rejected on the basis of mere empirical contingencies.

The current and still-waxing allure of the inequality hypothesis, we submit, lies not in its record of testable research results, but rather in the gravitational sway of its doctrine. Doctrine may attract believers and persuade converts entirely in the absence of fact and evidence. (The quintessence of doctrinal faith, indeed, is its immunity to empirical assault.) How the currently fashionable inequality hypothesis will fare in the years to come is beyond our ability to predict. In the final analysis, however, the inequality hypothesis itself appears to be a misnomer, for it is less accurate to describe it as a scientific hypothesis than a doctrine in search of data.

Notes

1. Richard G. Wilkinson, *Unhealthy Societies: The Affliction of Inequality* (London: Routledge, 1996).

2. *American Journal of Public Health* 87, no. 9 (1997).

3. Both its Socialist Caucus and Spirit of 1848 Caucus are devoted to redistribution of wealth in the name of health. The theme of the American Public Health Association's 1996 annual meeting was "Empowering the Disadvantaged: Social Justice in Public Health." Also see Sally Satel, M.D., "Public Health and the Quest for Social Justice," in *PC, M.D.: How Political Correctness Is Corrupting Medicine* (New York: Basic Books, 2000), 9–43.

4. National Program Report of the Investigator Awards in Health Policy Research. Available at http://www.rwjf.org/reports/npreports/investigatore.htm (accessed November 25, 2003).

5. John Lloyd, "Take a Dose of Socialism: Public Health and the UK," *New Statesman* 127, no. 4392 (1998): 11.

6. "Inequality, Poverty, and Socio-economic Performance: Inequality and Health," a list of articles dedicated to the inequality hypothesis. Available at www.worldbank.org/poverty/inequal/abstracts/health (accessed November 25, 2003).

7. M. Metzler, N. Keenan, and the CDC/ATSDR Social Determinants of Health Working Group, "Developing an Applied Social Determinants of Health Research and Practice Program at the U.S. Centers for Disease Control and Prevention" (Atlanta, Ga.: U.S. Centers for Disease Control and Prevention, 2002).

8. Erica Goode, "For Good Health, It Helps to Be Rich and Important," *New York Times,* June 1, 1999; Abigail Trafford, "Health and the Wealth Gap," *Washington Post,* May 18, 1999; Robert Pear, "Researchers Link Income Inequality to Higher Rates of Death," *New York Times,* April 19, 1996.

9. G. B. Rodgers, "Income and Inequality and Determinants of Mortality: An International Cross-Section Analysis," *Population Studies*

33 (1979): 343–51; J. M. Mellor and J. D. Milyo, "Insights Section," ed. E. Bardach, *Journal of Policy Analysis and Management* 20, no. 1 (2001): 151–59.

10. For an introduction to this position, see Vincente Navarro, "The Underdevelopment of Health or the Health of Underdevelopment: An Analysis of the Distribution of Human Health Resources in Latin America," *International Journal of Health Services* 4, no. 1 (1974): 5–27; Navarro, "The Crisis of the Western System of Medicine in Contemporary Capitalism," *International Journal of Health Services* 8, no. 2 (1978): 179–211; D. Coburn, "Income Inequality, Social Cohesion, and the Health Status of Populations: The Role of Neo-Liberalism," *Social Science and Medicine* 51, no. 1 (2000): 135–46.

11. Richard G. Wilkinson, "Income Distribution and Life Expectancy," *British Medical Journal* 304, no. 6820 (1992): 165–68.

12. These articles have been collected in Ichiro Kawachi, Bruce P. Kennedy, and Richard G. Wilkinson, eds., *The Society and Population Health Reader: Income Inequality and Health,* vol. 1 (New York: New Press, 1999).

13. Richard G. Wilkinson, "The Epidemiological Transition: From Material Scarcity to Social Disadvantage?" *Daedalus* 123 (1994): 61–77.

14. Wilkinson, *Unhealthy Societies,* 2–3.

15. Rodgers, "Income and Inequality and Determinants of Mortality," 343–51.

16. Ibid., 350.

17. A. T. Flegg, "Inequality of Income, Illiteracy and Medical Care as Determinants of Infant Mortality in Underdeveloped Countries," *Population Studies* 36, no. 3 (1982): 441–58; J. Le Grand, "Inequalities in Health," *European Economic Review* 31 (1987): 182–91; F. C. Pampel and V. K. Pillai, "Patterns and Determinants of Infant Mortality in Developed Nations, 1950–1975," *Demography* 23, no. 4 (1986): 525–42.

18. Le Grand, "Inequalities in Health," 189; see also A. Deaton, "Commentary: The Convoluted Story of International Studies of Inequality and Health," *International Journal of Epidemiology* 31, no. 3 (2002): 546–49; I. Wennemo, "Infant Mortality, Public Policy and Inequality: A Comparison of 18 Industrialized Countries, 1950–85," *Sociology of Health and Illness* 15 (1993): 429–46.

19. R. J. Waldmann, "Income Distribution and Infant Mortality," *Quarterly Journal of Economics* 107, no. 4 (1992): 1283–1302.

20. Norman Daniels, Bruce Kennedy, and Ichiro Kawachi, *Is Inequality Bad for Our Health?* (Boston: Beacon Press, 2000).

21. Ibid., 9.

22. Richard G. Wilkinson, "Commentary: Income Inequality Summarises the Health Burden of Individual Relative Deprivation," *British Medical Journal* 314, no. 7096 (1997): 1727–28; B. P. Kennedy et al., "Income Distribution, Socioeconomic Status, and Self Rated Health in the United States: Multilevel Analysis," *British Medical Journal* 317, no. 7163 (1998): 917–21; M. J. Soobader and F. B. LeClere, "Aggregation and the Measurement of Income Inequality: Effects on Morbidity," *Social Science and Medicine* 48, no. 6 (1999): 733–44.

23. Daniels, Kennedy, and Kawachi, *Is Inequality Bad,* 11.

24. Ibid., 12.

25. G. A. Kaplan et al., "Inequality in Income and Mortality in the United States: Analysis of Mortality and Potential Pathways," *British Medical Journal* 312, no. 7037 (1996): 999–1003.

26. B. P. Kennedy, I. Kawachi, and D. Prothrow-Stith, "Income Distribution and Mortality: Cross-Sectional Ecological Study of the Robin Hood Index in the United States," *British Medical Journal* 312 (1996): 1004–7.

27. Yoav Ben-Shlomo, I. R. White, and M. Marmot, "Does the Variation in the Socioeconomic Characteristics of an Area Effect Mortality?" *British Medical Journal* 312, no. 7037 (1996): 1013–14.

28. Ibid., 1014.

29. H. Gravelle, "How Much of the Relation Between Population Mortality and Unequal Distribution of Income Is a Statistical Artefact?" *British Medical Journal* 316, no. 7128 (1998): 382–85.

30. J. M. Mellor and J. D. Milyo, "Reexamining the Ecological Association Between Income Inequality and Health," *Journal of Health Politics, Policy and Law* 26, no. 3 (2001): 487–522.

31. Cited in T. Marmor, "Do Inequalities Matter?" *Boston Review* 25, no. 1 (2000): 13–15.

32. A. Deaton, "Inequalities in Income and Inequalities in Health," NBER Working Paper 7141 (Cambridge, Mass.: National Bureau of Economic Research, 1999); J. M. Mellor and J. D. Milyo, "Income Inequality and Individual Health: Evidence from the Current Population Survey," Robert Wood Johnson Health Policy Scholars Working Paper no. 8 (Boston: Boston University School of Management, 1999); Mellor and Milyo, "Reexamining the Ecological Association Between Income Inequality and Health," 487–522; K. Judge, "Income Distribution and Life Expectancy: A Critical Appraisal," *British Medical Journal* 311, no. 7015 (1995): 1282–85; K. Judge, J. Mulligan, and M. Benzeval, "Income Inequality and Population Health," *Social Science and Medicine* 46,

no. 4–5 (1998): 567–79; K. Fiscella and P. Franks, "Poverty or Income Inequality as Predictor of Mortality: Longitudinal Cohort Study," *British Medical Journal* 314, no. 7096 (1997): 1724–27; M. C. Daly et al., "Macro-to-Micro Links in the Relation Between Income Inequality and Mortality," *Milbank Quarterly* 76 (1998): 303–4, 315–39; Kennedy et al., "Income Distribution," 917–21; Soobader and LeClere, "Aggregation," 733–44; K. Fiscella and P. Franks, "Individual Income, Income Inequality, Health, and Mortality: What Are the Relationships?" *Health Service Research* 35, no. 1, pt. 2 (2000): 307–18; Jeffrey Milyo and Jennifer M. Mellor, "Is Income Inequality Bad for Your Health?" *Critical Review* 13, no. 3–4 (2000): 359–72. See also R. Sturm and C. R. Gresenz, "Relations of Income Inequality and Family Income and Their Relationships to Chronic Medical Conditions and Mental Health Disorders: National Survey," *British Medical Journal* 324, no. 7328 (2002): 20–23, in which the authors write, "No relation was found between income inequality and the prevalence of chronic medical problems or depressive disorders and anxiety disorders, either across the whole population or among poorer people." Other studies based their health measures on surveys employing self-reported general responses ("What would you say your health is: excellent, good, fair, poor?") or on aggregate mortality statistics. The analysis by Sturm and Gresenz is unique in employing information concerning specific medical and mental health problems. Also see J. Mellor and J. Milyo, "Income Inequality and Health Status in the United States: Evidence from the Current Population Survey," *Journal of Human Resources* 37, no. 3 (2002): 510–39; J. Mellor and J. Milyo, "Is Exposure to Income Inequality a Public Health Concern? Lagged Effects of Income Inequality on Individual and Population Health," *Health Services Research* 38, no. 1, pt. 1 (2003): 137–51; Ellen Meara, "Inequality and Infant Health" (Cambridge, Mass.: Harvard University, 1999, unpublished manuscript).

33. Mellor and Milyo, "Income Inequality and Health Status," 510–39; Mellor and Milyo, "Exposure to Income Inequality," 137–51.

34. Cited in Marmor, "Do Inequalities Matter?" 13–15.

35. The question is by no means an idle one. There is no reason for perceived or experienced "inequality" to fluctuate solely, or even primarily, in response to reported income differences. Japan offers the example of a nation with a relatively even distribution of income and, at the same time, a relatively strong social stricture that prevents mobility and opportunity for significant segments of the population (e.g., ethnic minorities, women). India's caste system provides another instance of a profoundly regimented system of stratification, hierarchy, and inequality

that resists the modern impetus to ascribe an individual's status according to his or her income. See Louis Dumont, *Homo Hierarchicus: The Caste System and Its Implication* (Chicago: University of Chicago Press, 1970.) Furthermore, as Angus Deaton has noted, prisons and armies illustrate cases where extreme inequalities of authority and power can coexist with extreme "income inequality." See Angus Deaton, "Health, Inequality and Economic Development," *Journal of Economic Literature* 41, no. 3 (March 2003): 113–58. The same point could also be made of Marxist-Leninist states. In all of these settings, after all, the distribution of authority is highly *unequal*—extremely concentrated—even though income or consumption levels tend to be quite even.

36. A. Muller, "Education, Income Inequality, and Mortality: A Multiple Regression Analysis," *British Medical Journal* 324, no. 7328 (2002): 23–25.

37. Ibid., 23.

38. Sturm and Gresenz, "Relations of Income Inequality," 20–23.

39. J. S. House, "Related Social Inequality in Health and Income," *Journal of Health Politics, Policy and Law* 26, no. 3 (2001): 523–30.

40. Ibid., 528.

41. W. S. Robinson, "Ecological Correlation and the Behavior of Individuals," *American Sociological Review* 15, no. 3 (1950): 357–61.

42. Fiscella and Franks, "Poverty or Income Inequality," 1724–28.

43. Ibid., 1727.

44. M. Osler et al., "Income Inequality, Individual Income, and Mortality in Danish Adults: Analysis of Pooled Data from Two Cohort Studies," *British Medical Journal* 324, no. 7328 (2002): 13–16.

45. Meara, "Inequality and Infant Health."

46. Mellor and Milyo, "Income Inequality and Health Status," 510–39.

47. A. Deaton and C. Paxson, "Mortality, Education, Income and Inequality among American Cohorts," in *Themes in the Economics of Aging,* ed. David A. Wise (Chicago: University of Chicago Press, 2001), 129–71.

48. James S. Coleman, "Social Capital in the Creation of Human Capital," *American Journal of Sociology* 94 (1998): 95–120. Social capital is a loose term describing the pattern and intensity of networks among people with shared values; its main aspects are citizenship, neighborliness, trust and shared values, community involvement, volunteering, social networks, and civic participation.

49. Pamela Paxton, "Is Social Capital Declining in the United States? A Multiple Indicator Assessment," *American Journal of Sociology* 105, no.1 (1999): 88–127.

50. Ibid.; Dora L. Costa and Matthew E. Kahn, "Understanding the Decline in Social Capital, 1952–1998" (unpublished paper, October 9, 2001).

51. See, for example, Richard Rose, "How Much Does Social Capital Add to Individual Health? A Survey Study of Russians," *Social Science and Medicine* 51, no. 9 (2000): 1421–35; Richard Rose, "The Impact of Social Capital on Health," University of Strathclyde Centre for the Study of Public Policy, *Studies in Public Policy* 358 (2001).

52. Francis Fukuyama, *Trust: The Social Virtues and the Creation of Prosperity* (New York: Free Press, 1995).

53. World Bank, *World Development Report 2003* (New York: Oxford University Press, 2003), 236–37.

54. U.S. Census Bureau, Historical Income Tables–Families, Table F-4: Gini Ratios for Families by Race and Hispanic Origin of Householder: 1947 to 2001. Available at http://www.census.gov/hhes/income/histinc/f04.html (accessed 17 November 2003).

55. Robert Putnam, *Bowling Alone: The Collapse and Revival of American Community* (New York: Simon and Schuster, 2000); Everett C. Ladd, "The Data Just Don't Show Erosion of America's 'Social Capital,'" *The Public Perspective* (June/July 1996): 1, 5–6; Dora L. Costa and Matthew E. Kahn, "Understanding the Decline in Social Capital, 1952-1998," NBER Working Papers, no. 8295 (2001); Pamela Paxton, "Is Social Capital Declining in The United States? A Multiple Indicators Assessment," *American Journal of Sociology* 108 (1999): 88–127.

56. Robert J. Waldmann, "Income Distribution and Infant Mortality," in Kawachi, Kennedy, and Wilkinson, *The Society and Population Health Reader*, 14.

57. Ibid.

58. John W. Lynch and George A. Kaplan, "Understanding How Inequality in the Distribution of Income Affects Health," in Kawachi, Kennedy, and Wilkinson, *The Society and Population Health Reader*, 212.

59. B. S. McEwen, "Protective and Damaging Effects of Stress Mediators," *New England Journal of Medicine* 338, no. 3 (1998): 171–79.

60. R. M. Sapolsky, S. C. Alberts, and J. Altmann, "Hypercortisolism Associated With Social Subordinance or Social Isolation Among Wild Baboons," *Archives of General Psychiatry* 54, no. 12 (1997): 1137–43.

61. Janice E. Williams et al., "Anger Proneness Predicts Coronary Heart Disease Risk: Prospective Analysis from the Atherosclerosis Risk

in Communities Study," *Circulation* 101, no. 17 (2000): 2034–39; C. Iribarren et al., "Association of Hostility with Coronary Artery Calcification in Young Adults: the CARDIA Study," *Journal of the American Medical Association* 283, no. 19 (2000): 2546–51.

62. Aron Wolfe Siegman, "Cardiovascular Consequences of Expressing and Repressing Anger," in Aron Wolfe Siegman and Timothy W. Smith eds., *Anger, Hostility, and the Heart* (Hillsdale, N.J.: Lawrence Erlbaum, 1994), 173–97.

63. Bruce S. McEwen, "Stress, Adaptation, and Disease: Allostasis and Allostatic Load," *Annals of the New York Academy of Sciences* 840 (1998): 33–44.

64. S. A. Everson et al., "Anger Expression and Incident Hypertension," *Psychosomatic Medicine* 60, no. 6 (1998): 730–35; S. B. Miller et al., "Dimensions of Hostility and Cardiovascular Response to Interpersonal Stress," *Journal of Psychosomatic Research* 41, no. 1 (1996): 91–95.

65. S. Leonard Syme, personal communication with Sally Satel, October 25, 1999.

66. S. Leonard Syme and Jennifer L. Balfour, "Social Determinants of Disease," in Robert B. Wallace, ed., *Public Health and Preventive Medicine,* 14th ed. (New York: McGraw-Hill, 1998), 795–810.

67. Robert G. Evans, Morris L. Barer, and Theodore R. Marmor, eds., *Why Are Some People Healthy and Others Not? The Determinants of Health of Populations* (New York: Aldine De Gruyter, 1994).

68. M. E. P. Seligman, *Helplessness: On Depression, Development and Death* (San Francisco: W H Freeman, 1975).

69. I. Kawachi and B. Kennedy, "Income Inequality and Health: Pathways and Mechanisms," *Health Service Research* 34, no. 1, pt. 2 (1999): 215–27; I. Kawachi and B. Kennedy, "Health and Social Cohesion: Why Care About Income Inequality?" *British Medical Journal* 314, no. 7086 (1997): 1037–40.

70. I. Kawachi et al., "Social Capital, Income Inequality and Mortality," *American Journal of Public Health* 87, no. 9 (1997): 1491–98.

71. Kawachi et al., "Social Capital," in Kawachi, Kennedy, and Wilkinson, *The Society and Population Health Reader,* 230.

72. Daniels, Kennedy, and Kawachi, *Is Inequality Bad,* 14.

73. Sapolsky, Alberts, and Altmann, "Hypercortisolism," 1137–43.

74. McEwen, "Protective and Damaging Effects," 171–79.

75. H. Uno et al., "Hippocampal Damage Associated with Prolonged and Fatal Stress in Primates," *Journal of Neuroscience* 9, no. 5 (1989): 1705–11; J. R. Kaplan et al., "Plaque Changes and Arterial Enlargement

in Atherosclerotic Monkeys after Manipulation of Diet and Social Environment," *Arteriosclerosis, Thrombosis and Vascular Biology* 13, no. 2 (1993): 254–63; C. A. Shively, M. B. Fontenot, and J. R. Kaplan, "Social Status, Behavior and Central Serotonergic Responsivity in Female Cynomolgus Monkeys," *American Journal of Primatology* 37 (1995): 333–39; S. W. Line et al., "Effects of Social Reorganization on Cellular Immunity in Male Cynomolgus Monkeys," *American Journal of Primatology* 39 (1996): 235–49; S. Cohen et al., "Chronic Social Stress, Social Dominance, and Susceptibility to Upper Respiratory Infections in Nonhuman Primates," *Psychosomatic Medicine* 59 (1997): 213–21; J. R. Kaplan et al., "Premenopausal Social Status and Hormone Exposure Predict Postmenopausal Atherosclerosis in Female Monkeys," *Obstetrics and Gynecology* 99, no. 3 (2002): 381–88; J. R. Kaplan et al., "Central Nervous System Monoamine Correlates of Social Dominance in Cynomolgus Monkeys (Macaca Fascicularis)," *Neuropsychopharmacology* 26 (2002): 431–43.

76. C. A. Shively and T. B. Clarkson, "Social Status and Coronary Artery Atherosclerosis in Female Monkeys," *Arteriosclerosis, Thrombosis and Vascular Biology* 14, no. 5 (1994): 721–26.

77. C. Shively et al., "Depression and Coronary Artery Atherosclerosis and Reactivity in Female Cynomolgus Monkeys," *Psychosomatic Medicine* 64 (2002): 699–706.

78. Shively and Clarkson, "Social Status and Coronary Artery Atherosclerosis," 721.

79. J. R. Kaplan and S. B. Manuck, "Status, Stress, and Atherosclerosis: the Role of Environment and Individual Behavior," *Annals New York Academic Science* 896 (1999): 145–61.

80. By contrast, subordinate animals did not seem greatly affected whether they remained in stable settings or were presented with a new male.

81. I. D. Chase et al., "Individual Differences versus Social Dynamics in the Formation of Animal Dominance Hierarchies," *Proceedings of the National Academy of Sciences* 99, no. 8 (2002): 5744–49.

About the Authors

Nicholas Eberstadt is the Henry Wendt Scholar in Political Economy at the American Enterprise Institute. He also serves on the Board of Scientific Counselors for the U.S. National Center for Health Statistics. Mr. Eberstadt has written widely on issues in demography, economic development, and international security. Mr. Eberstadt earned his AB, MPA, and PhD from Harvard, and his MSc from the London School of Economics.

Sally Satel, MD is a Resident Scholar at the American Enterprise Institute and staff psychiatrist at the Oasis Clinic in Washington, D.C. She graduated from the Brown University Program in Medicine and completed residency in psychiatry at Yale University, where she was also an assistant professor of psychiatry from 1988 to 1993. Dr. Satel has written extensively on drug addiction and the politicization of medicine and science. She is the author of *PC, M.D.: How Political Correctness Is Corrupting Medicine* (Basic Books, 2001).